LEVEL UP!

THE ULTIMATE GUIDE FOR BOYS 8-12

Cristiane Lobato

Copyright © 2025 Cristiane Lobato

Illustrated by Ricky Audi

ISBN 978-1-7641081-0-2 eBook
ISBN 978-1-7641081-1-9 Paperback

DEDICATION

To my amazing son, Nicolas Robert Lobato Cahill.

You are my greatest teacher and inspiration. This book is for you and for every boy who is growing up without a father to guide him. While I may never fill the space your father left, I promise to always be here, cheering you on, answering your questions, and walking beside you as you discover who you are.

With love,

Mum

CONTENTS

Introduction................................... vii

Chapter 1: **What's Happening to My Body?!**............. 1

Chapter 2: **Feelings—Why Are They So... Tricky?!**........ 9

Chapter 3: **Where Do I Belong? (Hint: Right Here!)**....... 15

Chapter 4: **Be the Boss of Your Body and Mind!**......... 21

Chapter 5: **Be Kind. Be Strong. Be You!**.............. 25

Chapter 6: **Let's Talk About Crushes**................ 31

Chapter 7: **Body Curiosity & Boundaries**............. 36

Chapter 8: **Handling Peer Pressure Like a Boss**......... 41

Chapter 9: **Making Good Choices & Taking Responsibility**.... 45

Chapter 10: **Online Safety & Navigating the Digital World**.... 49

Chapter 11: **Money & Responsibility Basics**........... 53

Chapter 12: **My Dad's Here... But Every Dad Is Different!**..... 58

Chapter 13: **Growing Up Without a Father**............ 63

Chapter 14: **Building a Strong Relationship with Mum & Other Supportive People**............ 69

INTRODUCTION

Hey there!

If you've ever had questions about growing up, your body, feelings, friendships, or just life in general—this book is for you! Maybe you've noticed changes happening to your body, maybe your emotions feel bigger than before, or maybe you just want to know how to feel more confident in who you are. Whatever it is, I want you to know that you're not alone.

I wrote this book because I know that growing up isn't always easy—especially when you don't have a dad around to help answer some of the big (and sometimes awkward) questions. But guess what? You don't need to figure it all out by yourself! Think of this book as your go to guide, packed with fun facts, helpful tips, and real talk about the stuff that matters.

This book is here to help you:

1. Understand your body and the changes that come with growing up
2. Learn how to deal with tricky emotions and build confidence
3. Figure out friendships, social skills, and standing up for yourself
4. Create healthy habits for your body and mind
5. Explore what it means to be a kind, strong, and awesome person
6. Learn about CRUSHES
7. Deal with your body sensations and personal space
8. Figure out what to do when someone is 'PUSHIE'
9. Make Good Choices & Take Responsibility
10. Navigate the Digital World
11. Become a $ boss
12. Every dad is different
13. Explore what it feels like to grow up without a Father
14. Build relationship with mum and other trusted adults

Bonus Features:

🚀 **Quizzes & Fun Challenges**

1. **What Kind of Awesome Dude Are You? Quiz** – A personality-style quiz help you to discover your strengths and what makes YOU unique.

2. **How Well Do You Know yourself? Challenge** – A fun self-reflection quiz about habits, emotions, and social skills.

3. **Level Up Your Life Game** – A checklist where YOU can tick off personal growth achievements like ' I helped someone today" or "I tried something new!'

4. **Crush-O-Meter: How Big Is Your Crush?**

5. **Friendship -Who's really got your back** – with an emergency kit friendship and What Kind of Friend Are You? QUIZZ

6. **Cool Printable Activities**

7. **Family System Domino Effect Game**

Every boy deserves to feel supported, informed, and proud of who he is. So, let's go on this journey together—you've got this!

CHAPTER 1
WHAT'S HAPPENING TO MY BODY?!

Hey, you! Yes, you—the awesome kid reading this book. Have you noticed anything... lately? Maybe you're growing taller, maybe your voice is doing weird squeaky things, or maybe your socks smell like they could knock out an elephant. Don't panic! You're not turning into a werewolf (probably). You're just going through puberty—aka, the time when your body starts growing into its next-level version: **a teenager.**

What Is Puberty, and Why Is It Messing With Me?

Puberty is like a *game update* for your body—it happens to **everyone,** but not always at the same time or in the same way. Your brain tells your body, "Okay, it's time to grow up!" and suddenly, BOOM—things start changing.

Here's what you might notice:

- ☑ You get taller (sometimes really fast!)
- ☑ Your voice starts cracking like a bad WiFi signal
- ☑ Hair starts growing in *new* places (armpits, face, down there...)
- ☑ Sweat happens. And yeah, it can get *stinky*
- ☑ Pimples might show up like surprise guests
- ☑ Your emotions feel all over the place—angry one minute, happy the next

You start thinking about crushes (yep, that's normal too!)

All of this is **TOTALLY NORMAL.** Your body is just getting ready for the next exciting stage of life.

Challenge #1: "I'm Growing Taller"

Ever feel like your arms and legs belong to a giraffe? That's because different parts of your body grow at different speeds. You might feel clumsy for a while—like you suddenly don't know how to walk without tripping over your own feet.

💡 **Solution:** Your body will catch up. If you keep bumping into things, try sports or activities that improve coordination, like swimming, basketball, or even skateboarding. And don't worry—this awkward phase won't last forever!

Challenge #2: "Why Do I Smell Like a Gym Locker?"

Ah, yes. Sweat. Before puberty, you probably didn't have to think much about smelling bad. But now? Your sweat glands are working overtime, and that means **body odour.**

💡 **Solution:** No big deal—just shower every day, use deodorant, and change your socks and underwear (*please*). Trust me, your future self (and everyone around you) will thank you!

Challenge #3: Pimples & Feeling Weird About Your Face

Alright, legend—let's talk about something that might already be happening or is about to: **PIMPLES.**

Yep, those little red bumps that seem to appear out of nowhere right when you're about to take the best selfie or go to a party.

Why do pimples happen?

Because your body is basically turning into a superhero-in-training right now. It's making something called **hormones**—kind of like secret codes that tell your body to grow, change, and… make extra oil on your skin. Sometimes that oil gets stuck, and BOOM—a pimple.

🐯 But What If Someone Makes Fun of Me?

Sometimes other kids tease because they don't understand that pimples are just a normal part of growing up. Here's the truth:

EVERYONE gets pimples.

Even that "cool" kid teasing you? His volcano zit is probably waiting around the corner.

🧩 What to Do If You Feel Self-Conscious

Self-conscious is when you feel awkward, embarrassed, or weird about how you look. That feeling is normal, but it doesn't have to run the show. Here's your power-up plan:

Wash your face every day. Use a simple, gentle face wash—not too scrubby.

- **Don't pop pimples!** It can make them worse and leave marks.
- **Talk to someone.** A parent, older cousin, or even your school counsellor. They've all been there.
- **Flip the script.** Next time someone teases you, hit them with this: *"Oh yeah? I'm just unlocking my Teen Mode early. What level are you on?"*
- **Focus on your awesome skills.** Remember: You're more than a pimple. You're funny, kind, clever, and learning cool stuff every day.

🧘 Quick Self-Talk Cheat Code

Whenever you're feeling down about your skin, press this mental button: *"Pimples don't define me. I'm growing, learning, and leveling up to be an amazing human."*

💡 **TIP:** Wash your face daily with a gentle cleanser, drink water, and don't pick at pimples (I know it's tempting, but it makes them worse!). If acne gets really bad, a doctor or pharmacist can help.

Challenge #4: "My Voice Sounds Like a Broken Robot"

One second, you sound normal. The next, your voice cracks like a squeaky toy. This happens because your vocal cords are growing. It might feel embarrassing, but guess what? **Every guy goes through it.**

💡 **Solution:** Just roll with it. Laugh it off if your voice cracks during a sentence—it'll even out soon!

Challenge #5: "Why Do I Feel So Many Emotions at Once?"

Some days, you might feel **super confident.** Other days, you might feel annoyed for no reason. Puberty brings a *rollercoaster* of emotions because your brain is adjusting to new hormones.

💡 **Solution:** When you feel overwhelmed, take a deep breath. Do something that helps you chill—drawing, listening to music, playing outside. And if you need to talk, find someone you trust (your mum, a friend, a teacher). You don't have to figure everything out alone.

Now after 5 CHALLENGES I believe you are ready for the "HAIRY" part:

Will I Be Hairy?! (A Family Investigation)

One day, you might look down at your arms, legs, or even your face and think, *Wait... was that always there?!* Congratulations—body hair is on its way! Some guys grow **a little**, some grow **a LOT**, and some look like they're turning into a werewolf (*okay, not really, but close*).

What's Happening to My Body?!

But here's a fun way to figure out what's coming—*investigate your family tree!*

💡 **Family Hair Detective:**

- Take a look at your **dad, uncles, grandfathers**, or even older brothers (*if you have them*).
- Now check out your **mum's side of the family** too—your genes come from both sides!
- Are the men in your family **hairy or smooth**? Did their beards grow fast or take *forever*?
- Ask them funny questions like, *"When did your first moustache hair appear?"* or *"Did you ever have an eyebrow that tried to take over your whole face?"*

You might even hear some hilarious stories—like the time your uncle tried to shave for the first time and ended up with a *massive* shaving cream disaster (*RIP to that bathroom mirror*).

👉 **Takeaway:** Whether you end up smooth, super hairy, or somewhere in between, **it's all normal!** Your body has a plan, and it's following the **family blueprint**—so sit back and enjoy the ride.

🌙 **Wet Dreams - Night-Time Surprises**

Now that we've had some fun with body hair and family traits, let's talk about something else that might pop up (pun intended) as your body starts levelling up.

At some point between about 9 and 14 years old (yep, it's different for everyone), your body might start making **sperm**. This is totally normal and just means puberty is in full swing. One way your body gets rid of some of that sperm is through something called a wet dream.

Here's what that means: you might wake up and notice your underwear or sheets are wet or sticky around your private parts. Don't worry, this doesn't mean you wet the bed or did anything wrong. It just means your body's doing a little "overnight maintenance."

Think of it as your body sending a message:

"All systems go, Captain! Everything's working just fine!"

☞ Fun fact: Wet dreams usually happen while you're sleeping, but sometimes a release can happen when you're awake, like if you're daydreaming, relaxed, or just hanging out. That's called a spontaneous ejaculation. Also normal. Also no big deal.

☞ What if it happens at school?

Okay, this is rare, but let's be real, it can happen. If it does, take a deep breath. It's usually not obvious to anyone else. Quietly ask to go to the bathroom, clean yourself up as best you can, and if you need to, go to the nurse or office. Most schools have a spare pair of undies or shorts for surprises—yep, even this kind.

💡 Also important: Not everyone gets wet dreams, and some boys don't notice when they happen. That's totally okay. Your body has its own unique timeline, and it's not a competition.

So if it happens? Just shower, change your undies, and move on.

🏆 **No drama. No shame. Just one more sign you're becoming awesome.**

The Bottom Line: You've Got This!

Puberty is weird, wild, and sometimes *a little or extremely awkward.* But remember—**everyone goes through it!** Your body is just doing its job, and you are becoming stronger, taller, and more *you* every day.

Stay curious, take care of yourself, and most importantly—**be proud of who you are.** You're growing into someone pretty amazing!

CHAPTER 2

FEELINGS—WHY ARE THEY SO... TRICKY?!

Alright, let's be real—emotions can be *weird.* One minute, you're totally fine, the next, you're mad at your shoelaces for coming undone (*seriously, why do they do that?!*). Sometimes, you don't even know why you feel the way you do. Welcome to the world of feelings—messy, confusing, and completely normal.

Why Do I Feel So Many Things at Once?

Imagine your emotions are like a **group chat** in your brain. Some days, everyone's getting along. Other days, Anger is yelling in ALL CAPS, Sadness is posting sad song lyrics, and Excitement is sending memes at 3 AM. It's chaos. But guess

what? **You're the admin.** You don't have to let your emotions take over—you can manage them.

Challenge #1: "I Get Angry Over the Smallest Things"

Your little brother *breathes* too loudly? Someone takes your seat? Suddenly, you're boiling inside! Anger isn't bad—it's just your brain saying, *"Hey! Something's not okay!"* But how you handle it matters.

💡 Solution:

- [x] Take a deep breath (*seriously, it helps*).
- [x] Move your body—walk, stretch, or punch a pillow (NOT your little brother).
- [x] Ask yourself, *"Is this really worth my energy?"* If not, let it go. If yes, find a calm way to talk about it.

Challenge #2: "I Feel Sad, But I Don't Know Why"

Sometimes, sadness is loud (*like when your team loses a big game*), but other times, it sneaks in quietly. You might feel *meh* for no reason. That's normal. Sadness usually means you need a little extra care.

💡 Solution:

- [x] Do something that makes you happy—hug your pet (*if you have one, if not, hug a pillow—it works too*).
- [x] Talk to someone you trust. You are not alone in this.
- [x] Remind yourself that feelings come and go—this won't last forever.

Challenge #3: "Sometimes, I Feel Like I'm Not Good Enough"

Ever feel like everyone else is better, cooler, or smarter? That's called **self-doubt,** and it's a *liar.* Your brain sometimes tells you stories that aren't true, like "I'm not good enough" or "I'll never be as cool as that guy." Let's rewrite those stories.

💡 **Solution:**

- ☑ Think of one thing you're *awesome* at (drawing, making people laugh, building epic Lego towers—anything!).
- ☑ Instead of "I'm not good at this," say, "I'm still learning." **(Nobody starts out perfect.)**
- ☑ Surround yourself with people who make you feel good about yourself.

☞ **Tip:** Confidence isn't about being the *best*, it's about accepting yourself as you are. And guess what? You're already pretty great.

Challenge #4: "I Worry About Everything"

What if I fail my test? What if I say something dumb? What if an asteroid hits the Earth tomorrow?! (Okay, probably not gonna happen, but still!) Worrying is your brain's way of trying to protect you, but too much of it can make life stressful.

💡 **Solution:** ☑ Write down your worry. Then ask, "Is this something I can control?"

☑ If yes, make a plan. If no, let it go (easier said than done, but it gets better with practice!).

☀ **Here's the trick with your plan:** When you decide to make a plan, check first:

- **Can I fix it?** (Like studying a bit more for my test.)
- **Can I change it?** (Like apologising if I said something dumb.)
- **Can I prepare for it?** (Like learning how to handle if someone laughs at me.)

If the answer is YES → Make your plan and take action. If the answer is NO → Hit the «Let It Go» button in your brain. Worrying won't change it, so don't waste your awesome energy on it.

☑ Picture the worst-case scenario, then ask yourself, "Would I survive that?"

The answer is usually YES. You're stronger than your worries!

The Confidence Secret No One Tells You

Ready? Here it is: **Confident people aren't fearless. They just don't let fear stop them.**

Confidence isn't about always knowing what to do. It's about trying, even when you're unsure. It's about knowing you won't always get it right—and that's okay.

So next time you feel nervous, remember **you are capable, strong, and totally enough—just as you are.**

Final Takeaway: Emotions = Superpowers

Imagine if superheroes never felt emotions. No sadness, no fear, no excitement. *Boring, right?* Your emotions make you *you.* They help you grow, connect, and learn about yourself. The trick is learning how to **use them,** not letting them control you.

So, next time your "group chat" of feelings gets loud, take a deep breath, step back, and remember: **You're in charge.** And you? **You've got this.**

CHAPTER 3

WHERE DO I BELONG?
(HINT: RIGHT HERE!)

Ever walked into a room and felt like *everyone else* belonged except you? Maybe you weren't sure where to sit at lunch, or you wondered if your friends really *get* you. Well, here's the truth: **You belong.** Full stop. No one gets left out in life—you have a place, and it's yours to take.

Let's talk about how to **find your people, make friendships work, and stand up for yourself when needed.**

Belonging: It's Like a Puzzle

Imagine a giant puzzle. Every piece is shaped differently, but they *all* fit together to make the full picture. That's how life works! You don't have to be the same as everyone else—you just have to **be yourself and find your fit.**

If you're here, you belong. It doesn't matter where you were born, what your family looks like, or if you feel "different" sometimes. **The fact that you exist means you have a place.**

☞ **Lesson #1: Stop waiting for an invite—claim your space.** You don't need permission to belong. Walk into the room like you're meant to be there (because you are).

Friendships: Finding Your People

Not everyone will be *your* person—and that's okay. Some people like pineapple on pizza (*weird*), some don't. The key is to find friends who **see the real you** and make you feel good about yourself.

💡 **How to Find Your Crew:**

- [x] Look for people who like the same things as you (*gaming, sports, weird science facts*).
- [x] Be yourself—people can tell when you're faking it.
- [x] Notice how you *feel* around them—do they lift you up or bring you down?

💡 **How to Be a Great Friend:**

- [x] Listen as much as you talk.
- [x] Cheer for their wins, even when it's not your turn to shine.

- [x] Say sorry when you mess up (everyone does sometimes).

Not every friendship lasts forever, and that's normal too. Some friends are here for a season, some for a lifetime. Either way, **you'll always find new people who get you.**

Challenge #1: "I Feel Left Out"

Maybe your friends made plans without you, or maybe you're in a new place where you don't know anyone yet. Feeling left out **hurts,** but it doesn't mean you don't belong—it just means it's time to take action.

💡 **Solution:**

- [x] **Check your inner voice.** Instead of "Nobody likes me," try, "I haven't found my people yet—but I will."
- [x] **Start the conversation.** Instead of waiting to be included, invite someone to play a game!
- [x] **Find different groups.** You don't need just *one* best friend—having a few different friendships makes life more fun.

👉 **Life Tip:** Sometimes, feeling left out is an *old story* playing in your head—maybe from a time you *actually* weren't included. But the past doesn't decide your future. **This is your life now—step in.**

Challenge #2: "What If People Don't Like Me?"

Quick reality check: Not everyone will like you. And that's FINE. You don't like everyone either, right? But that doesn't mean you don't belong—it just means you haven't found the right people yet.

💡 **Solution:**

- ☑ **Focus on who DOES like you.** The right people will stick around.
- ☑ **Remember: Someone else's opinion doesn't change your worth.**
- ☑ **Stand tall.** The way you carry yourself tells the world, *I belong here.* (Try it!)

Standing Up for Yourself (Without Being a Jerk)

One day, someone's going to say or do something that makes you feel small. Maybe they tease you, put you down, or try to push you aside. Here's what you do:

💡 **How to Stand Up for Yourself:**

- ☑ **Use your voice.** A calm, "That's not okay" is more powerful than shouting.
- ☑ **Set boundaries.** If someone keeps crossing the line, walk away—your energy is too valuable.
- ☑ **Ask for backup.** If it gets serious, tell an adult or a trusted friend.

Standing up for yourself doesn't mean being aggressive—it just means knowing your worth and **not letting anyone treat you like you don't matter.** Because you *do.*

Final Takeaway: You Already Belong

You don't need to *change* to fit in. You don't need to be louder, quieter, cooler, or anything else. **You are enough exactly as you are.** Your people are out there, and the more you step into your space, the more they'll find you.

So go ahead—grab your space, take up room, and **own your place in this world.** Because if you're here, you belong.

CHAPTER 4

BE THE BOSS OF YOUR BODY AND MIND!

Okay, real talk—your body and mind are like a superhero team. If you take care of them, **they'll take care of you.** But how do you actually *do* that without turning into a boring "health robot" who only eats broccoli and meditates all day?

Simple: **Find what works for you!**

Will You Follow the Family Habits… or Be a Health Champion?

Every family has habits—some good, some *not so good.* Maybe your grandma swears by early morning walks, or your dad can make a smoothie *with his eyes closed.* But maybe… your family's idea of exercise is reaching for the TV remote (*oops!*).

💡 **You have two choices:**

- ✔ **Follow the good habits** of your parents or grandparents (*thanks for the tips, Mum!*)
- ✔ **Start your own healthy traditions** and become the *first* in your family to kickstart it.

👉 **Either way, YOU win.** Your body and mind will thank you, whether you're keeping old traditions or creating new ones!

Challenge: But I Don't Like "Healthy Stuff"

Let's be honest—sometimes, healthy habits sound *boring* (or taste weird). But guess what? **Being healthy doesn't mean eating dry lettuce and running marathons.** It means finding cool ways to feel your best!

💡 **Here's how to make it fun:**

🏃 **Hate running?** Try skateboarding, dancing, or jumping on a trampoline instead.

🥬 **Not a fan of veggies?** Make a challenge: "How many colours can I eat today?" (Bonus: Green = superhero fuel.)

🧘 **Think mindfulness is weird?** Try a "1-minute chill break" after school—just breathe and see how different you feel.

Healthy habits aren't *rules*—they're just tricks to help you feel **stronger, happier, and ready to take on anything.**

The 3 Power-Ups of Healthy Habits

◉ Power-Up #1: Your Body Feels Good

- More energy, better focus, and fewer days feeling *blah*.
- Less chance of getting sick (*bonus: no missing out on fun stuff!*).

◉ Power-Up #2: Your Mind Stays Sharp

- Less stress, more confidence, and fewer random mood swings.
- You'll handle tricky situations like a pro (*goodbye, meltdowns*).

◉ Power-Up #3: You Set Yourself Up for Life

- The habits you build NOW will help you forever.
- You'll be the *wise* adult who says, *"Back in my day, I started drinking water before it was cool."*

Final Takeaway: You're in Charge

Healthy habits are like superpowers—you get to choose **how** you use them. Will you follow the good ones from your family? Will you be the *first* to start new ones? Either way, **you've got this!**

So go ahead—build those habits, have fun with them, and **become the healthiest version of YOU.** 🚀

CHAPTER 5

BE KIND. BE STRONG. BE YOU!

What makes someone **awesome**? Muscles? Super smarts? Being the fastest runner?

Nope.

The **most awesome people** are the ones who are kind, strong, and know their worth. And guess what? You can be **that person**—starting *right now*.

But before you go saving the world (*or at least your little corner of it*), you need to start with **yourself.**

Step 1: Be Kind to YOU First

Would you ever tell your best friend, *"You're not good enough"*

or *"You'll never get better at this"*? NO WAY! That would be mean! But sometimes, we **say these things to ourselves** without even realising it.

💡 **Challenge:** Pay attention to your self-talk this week.

- ✓ **If you mess up,** say, "That's okay, I'll try again."
- ✓ **If you feel bad about something,** remind yourself, "Everyone has tough days—it doesn't mean I'm not awesome."
- ✓ **If you succeed,** celebrate! Give yourself a mental high-five.

Being kind to yourself doesn't mean being lazy or making excuses—it means **treating yourself like someone worth cheering for.** (Because you ARE!)

Step 2: How Your Actions Affect Others

Imagine you're playing a game, and your teammate messes up. You can either:

- Roll your eyes and say, "Wow, thanks for losing the game for us."
- Say, "No worries, we'll get it next time!"

One of those choices makes the person feel awful. The other helps them bounce back and try again.

Every **word** you say and every **action** you take has a ripple effect—like a stone in a pond. You don't have to be perfect, but **you can choose to be the kind of person who lifts people up instead of bringing them down.**

💡 **Try This:**

- ✓ **Notice how people react to your words.** Are they smiling or shrinking away? Or shouting back at you?
- ✓ **Think before you speak.** Would YOU like to hear what you're about to say?
- ✓ **Give compliments!** A simple "Hey, nice job" can make someone's whole day better.

Step 3: Giving and Taking—Kindness Goes Both Ways

Being kind is awesome, but let's get real: **not everyone is kind back.**

💡 **If you had a friend who kept going back to a place where they were mistreated, wouldn't you tell them to leave?** Well, you need to do the same for yourself.

- ✓ **Kindness is a two-way street.** You don't have to be friends with people who treat you badly.
- ✓ **You can be kind and still walk away.** If someone doesn't respect you, **step back.**
- ✓ **Find your own tribe.** There are people out there who will appreciate you—stick with them!

☞ **You deserve to be around people who treat you well.** Being strong means knowing when to stay and when to walk away.

Step 4: Being Kind vs. Being a Doormat

Being kind does NOT mean saying "yes" to everything or letting people **walk all over you**. That's not kindness—that's letting people **take advantage** of you.

💡 **The Difference:**

- ✔ **Being kind:** Helping a friend when you WANT to.
- ✘ **Being a doormat:** Always saying yes, even when you don't want to.
- ✔ **Being considerate:** Letting your friend borrow your pen.
- ✘ **Being a doormat:** Letting them take all your stuff because you're afraid to say no.
- ✔ **Being strong and kind:** Standing up for yourself while staying respectful.
- ✘ **Being walked over:** Letting people treat you badly without speaking up.

👉 **Remember:** Kindness includes being kind to YOURSELF. If something feels unfair, **you're allowed to say no.**

Final Takeaway: You're Already Awesome!

Being kind, strong, and awesome isn't about being perfect. It's about:

- 🫶 Treating yourself with respect.
- 💪 Standing up for yourself when needed.
- ✨ Lifting others up instead of putting them down.

When you live like this, **people notice.** You'll be the kind of person that others **trust, respect, and look up to.** And that, my friend, is what makes someone **truly awesome.** 🚀

CHAPTER 6
LET'S TALK ABOUT CRUSHES

(Because Feelings Can Be Weird, but That's Totally Okay)

What Even Is a Crush?

- A **crush** is when you **really like someone in a special way**.
- It's different from liking a friend—it's when you feel excited, nervous, or just **want to be around that person more**.
- Crushes **aren't just about looks**—sometimes you like someone because they're funny, kind, or just cool to be around.

How Do You Know If You Have a Crush?

- Do you **want to talk to them more than other people?**
- Do you feel **a little nervous or awkward around them?**
- Do you **think about them when they're not around?**
- Do you **feel happy when they notice you?**
- If you answered yes to any of these, congrats! You might have a **crush!** 😄

Why Crushes Are Totally Normal?

- EVERYONE gets crushes (even adults!) It's a normal part of growing up.
- Some boys **might not have a crush yet**—and that's normal too! There's no rush.
- Having a crush **doesn't mean you have to do anything about it**. It's okay to just **enjoy the feeling and let it be**.

What If My Crush Doesn't Like Me Back? 😳

- **Ouch, that can hurt.** But guess what? It happens to EVERYONE at some point.
- You are **still awesome** even if someone doesn't like you back.
- **Crushes come and go.** The way you feel now won't last forever!

Do I Have to Tell Anyone?

- Nope! Your feelings are **your business**.
- Some people like talking about their crushes with friends, but you don't have to.
- If friends pressure you to say who you like, **you can keep it private**—just smile and say, "Nah, I'm good."

What If I Have a Crush on a Boy?

- That's okay too! Some boys like girls, some like boys, and some aren't sure yet.
- You don't have to figure it all out right now—just be yourself.

Respecting Other People's Feelings

(Because Nobody Likes Being Teased About a Crush)

- **Don't make fun of friends for their crushes**—how would you feel if someone teased you?
- **If someone tells you who they like, keep it private**—it's not your news to spread.
- **No means no.** If someone doesn't like you back, respect that—being pushy isn't cool.
- **It's okay to be curious, but don't pressure anyone to talk about their feelings.**

Final Thought: It's All Good!

- Crushes **should be fun, not stressful**.
- If you have a crush, cool! If you don't, also cool!
- Just remember—**you're still the same awesome YOU, no matter what!**

CHAPTER 7
BODY CURIOSITY & BOUNDARIES

(Because Your Body is Yours, and That's Pretty Awesome!)

Why Am I So Curious About My Body? 🫣

- As you grow up, you **start noticing more about your body**—how it looks, how it feels, and how it changes.
- You might **wonder about different body parts** or **want to explore how they work**—this is totally normal!
- All kids go through this phase, and **curiosity is just part of growing up**.

Your Body = Your Personal Space 🛑

- There's a simple rule: **Your body belongs to YOU.**
- It's okay to explore your body in **private**, but there are some important things to remember:
  - ◇ **Privacy means being alone in a safe space** (like your bedroom or bathroom).
  - ◇ **No one should be watching or involved—only you.**
  - ◇ **Touching other people's bodies or letting them touch yours is NOT okay.**

The "No Touching Others" Rule

- Just like **your body is yours**, other people's bodies belong to them.
- Even if you're curious, **it's NEVER okay to touch someone else's private parts**—and they should not touch yours.
- If someone ever tries to touch you in a way that makes you uncomfortable, **tell a safe adult you trust**.

Who is a Safe Adult?

A **safe adult** is someone who listens, protects, and respects your feelings. This could be:

- ☑ A parent or guardian
- ☑ A teacher or school counsellor
- ☑ A trusted family member
- ☑ A doctor (with your parent present)

🚨 **If someone tells you to keep a "secret" about touching, that is NOT okay.** Safe adults never ask you to keep unsafe secrets.

When is it Okay for Someone Else to See or Touch My Body?

There are very few times when another person might need to see or touch your body:

- **Doctors** may check your body, but only with a parent there and only for medical reasons.
- **Parents or caregivers** might help when you're little (like with bathing), but as you grow, privacy is important.
- **No one else** should be touching your private parts—**even if they say it's a game or a secret.**

Respecting Other People's Privacy

- Just like you want privacy, **others do too!**
- **Knock on doors before entering someone's room or the bathroom.**
- **Don't ask personal questions about someone else's body.**
- **Never make fun of someone's body—it's just not cool.**

Final Thought: You Are in Charge of Your Own Body!

- **Curiosity is normal**, but privacy is important.
- **You are the boss of your own body**—no one else.
- If something feels **wrong or weird**, **talk to a safe adult**—you're never alone.

CHAPTER 8

HANDLING PEER PRESSURE LIKE A BOSS

(Because Sometimes Friends Say Weird Things)

What is Peer Pressure?

- It's when friends (or classmates) **make you feel like you HAVE to do something to fit in**.
- This can be about **clothes, sports, video games, crushes, or even talking about "boy stuff"** like puberty, dating, and kissing.
- Sometimes, it's harmless fun—other times, it makes you uncomfortable.

"Wait, You Haven't Kissed Anyone Yet?" (And Other Silly Questions)

- Some boys might **brag about things that aren't even true** (like having a girlfriend or kissing someone).
- If you're not into that stuff yet (or ever), **that's okay!**
- **There's no "right time" for anything**—you do things when (and if) you feel ready.

How to Say "No" Without Making it Awkward

(Because Saying "Leave Me Alone" Isn't Always Easy)

- **Change the subject:** "Hey, did you see that insane goal in the game last night?"
- **Use humour:** "Yeah, I'm saving my first kiss for when I'm a billionaire."
- **Be direct (but chill):** "Not really my thing right now."
- **Walk away if needed:** Real friends won't force you to do stuff you don't want to do.

Online Peer Pressure: Social Media & Group Chats

- Some kids **post things to look cool** (or make others feel left out).
- **You don't have to follow the crowd**—you're not missing out just because you're not doing what they are.
- Be careful with **group chats**—don't feel forced to comment on things that feel uncomfortable.

- **If something online feels wrong, trust your gut and step away.**

The Real Flex? Being Yourself!

- **Coolest thing you can do?** Be confident in who YOU are.
- **Not everyone is ready for the same things at the same time.**
- **True friends won't pressure you—they'll respect your choices.**

CHAPTER 9

MAKING GOOD CHOICES & TAKING RESPONSIBILITY

Life Is Like a Video Game—You're Leveling Up!

Imagine you're playing your favourite game—let's say *Minecraft* or *Fortnite*. Every time you make a move, there's a reaction. If you build a strong base, you survive longer. If you run straight into danger without a plan, you lose health (or worse—GAME OVER!) The choices you make in the game shape what happens next. Well, guess what? **Real life works the same way.**

Your Brain = The Ultimate Controller (But It's Still Updating!)

Did you know that the part of your brain that helps you make smart choices—your *prefrontal cortex*—is **not fully developed until you're around 24 to 28 years old**? Yep! That means sometimes, making the right decision can be tricky. It's like

trying to beat a super hard level in a game **without** all the power-ups unlocked yet. That's why you need a good team—parents, teachers, mentors—to **help guide you until you're ready to take full control**.

Think about it this way:

Would you hand over the controller to a **toddler** to play your hardest level? No way! They'd probably press random buttons, mess up your stats, and get you eliminated in seconds. That's why it's totally okay to **ask adults for advice** when making big decisions—they've played the "game of life" longer and can help you avoid rookie mistakes.

Making Mistakes = Learning & Leveling Up

Here's the thing—**everyone makes mistakes**. Even adults! The trick is to learn from them so you can level up. Think about when you're playing a game:

🎮 You miss a jump and fall into lava—ouch! But next time, you calculate it better.

🎮 You craft the wrong item—whoops! Now you know what materials to use.

🎮 You trust the wrong teammate, and they betray you—lesson learned! That doesn't mean you should never trust anyone again. It just means now you know how to spot the signs when someone isn't being a real friend. Next time, you'll choose your teammates more carefully!

In real life, mistakes work the same way. If you mess up, **own it, learn from it, and move forward.** That's how you get stronger and more unstoppable.

How to Make Smarter Choices (And Win at Life!)

- ✔ **Pause & Think** – Before making a decision, take a second to ask, *"What could happen if I do this?"* If the answer is **bad consequences**, rethink it!
- ✔ **Learn from Others** – Watch how older people (parents, mentors, even YouTubers) handle tough situations. You can pick up great strategies.
- ✔ **Own Your Mistakes** – If you mess up, don't blame others. Admit it, fix it, and move on—just like you would if you lost a match because of a bad play.
- ✔ **Know When to Ask for Help** – If something feels too overwhelming, talk to a trusted adult. Even pro gamers ask for tips when they're stuck!

Final Power-Up:

Mistakes don't define you. **How you handle them does.** Every choice you make shapes your future—so make the best ones you can and keep leveling up!

CHAPTER 10

ONLINE SAFETY & NAVIGATING THE DIGITAL WORLD

The Internet: A Cool Tool or a Sneaky Trap?

Let's be real—the internet is **awesome**. You can game with friends, watch funny videos, and even learn new skills. But just like in your favourite games, there are **hidden dangers** and **tricky traps** that can catch you if you're not paying attention.

Think of the online world like a massive open-world game—there are **safe zones** and **danger zones**. The trick is **knowing how to navigate it safely,** so you don't end up in a bad situation.

Red Flags: When Your Body Tells You "Something's Off"

Your body is **smarter than you think**. Ever felt your stomach tighten when you were doing something you *knew* wasn't the best idea? Maybe you started sweating or felt nervous? **That's your body's alarm system going off.** If you ever feel like:

- ▶ "I hope my parents don't find out I'm doing this."
- ▶ "Something about this person/message/game feels weird."
- ▶ "I'm feeling pressured to send or say something I don't want to."

Then guess what? **It's probably not good for you.** When that alarm goes off, **listen to it** and take action. As the old saying goes, trust your gut.

When to Talk to an Adult (Even if You Think They'll Freak Out!)

I get it—sometimes you might think, *If I tell Mum or Dad, they're going to lose it!* But here's the deal:

- **It's better to deal with a little bit of yelling than to be in real trouble.**
- **Your safety matters more than a broken rule.**
- **If your parents are too upset, find another trusted adult—an older sibling, a teacher, or a family friend.**

No matter what, **you're never alone**, and there's always someone who can help you figure things out.

What's Real & What's Fake? (Don't Get Tricked!)

Not everything you see online is real. People can fake pictures, edit messages, and even pretend to be someone they're not. Here's how to spot some of the biggest **online traps**:

🕵 **Strangers Who Want "Secrets"** – If someone online tells you to keep a secret from your parents, 🚨 **BIG RED FLAG!** 🚨 Never share personal info like your school, address, or photos with someone you don't know in real life.

🎭 **Perfect-Looking People & Fake Lives** – Social media is full of people **only posting their best moments**. No one shows their bad days, messy hair, or boring homework. Don't compare yourself to something that isn't even real!

🔍 **Clickbait & Scams** – If something looks too good to be true (*"Click here for a free iPhone!"*), it's **probably a trap**. Don't fall for it.

The "Smart Player" Rules of the Internet

- ▶ Only friend/message people you actually know in real life.
- ▶ Don't click weird links or download sketchy stuff even if you really want that phone, music, movie, etc.
- ▶ Think before you post—would you want your grandma to see this?
- ▶ If something feels off, log out & tell an adult.

The online world **isn't going anywhere**, but if you **play smart**, you can enjoy it safely—just like a pro gamer who knows how to avoid the traps.

CHAPTER 11
MONEY & RESPONSIBILITY BASICS—BECOMING A MONEY BOSS!

What's the Deal with Money?

Money is pretty cool—it helps you buy the things you need and want. But here's the secret: learning how to handle money now will make you a pro at it when you're older. Think of it like a video game. You start at **Level 1: Pocket Money**, and as you learn to manage it, you level up to bigger, better things!

Three Money Rules Every Kid Should Know

- **Earn It** – Money doesn't appear out of nowhere! You can find fun ways to earn it.

- **Save It** – If you keep spending it all at once, you won't have any left for big things.
- **Spend It Wisely** – It's okay to buy fun things, but saving money and planning ahead is even smarter!

Level 1: Earning Money—It's Not Just About Chores!

Want to make a little extra cash? Here are some fun ideas:

- **Lemonade Stand? Nah, Try a Cool Drink Stand!** – Make flavoured waters, iced tea, or smoothies and sell them at a local event or to neighbours.
- **Trade or Sell Your Old Toys and Games** – Not playing with that LEGO set anymore? Sell it and put the money toward something new.
- **Book Swap Sale** – Got books you've outgrown? Organise a mini book sale with friends and trade or sell them.
- **The Plant Boss** – Grow small plants (like succulents or herbs) and sell them in decorated pots.
- **Pet Helper** – Walk a neighbour's dog or feed their cat while they're away.

Level 2: Spending Smart—What Will You Do with Your Money?

Here's where things get fun. You don't have to spend money right away—think about what would be the most rewarding!

- **Save up for a bigger reward** – Instead of buying snacks every week, maybe you save up for a game or a cool experience.
- **Try a "Spending Challenge"** – Can you make

$10 last all week? What's the most creative way to stretch your money?

- **Buy & Flip** – Find things at a garage sale or second-hand store, clean them up, and sell them for a profit.

💡 **Money Tip:** Every time you want to buy something, ask yourself, *"Will I still love this in a month?"*

Level 3: Learning to Let Go—Making Space for the New

Holding onto old things can keep you stuck in the past. Try these fun ways to **"trade in" the old for the new:**

- **The 2-for-1 Rule** – For every two things you sell or donate, you can get one new thing.
- **Give & Receive** – Give away toys you don't play with anymore to younger kids. It makes room for new experiences!
- **Room Makeover Challenge** – Sell old stuff and use the money to redecorate or buy something useful.

Level 4: The Boss Move—Giving Back

A real money pro knows that **sharing** is powerful. Even a small amount can make a big difference.

- ☑ **Donate a tiny part** of what you earn to a cause you care about.
- ☑ **Use your skills** to help others—if you're great at something, share your talent!

Final Level: The "Money Boss" Challenge

💡 Pick a challenge:

- **Earn $20 in a month and decide how to use it!**
- **Find something old to sell and make space for something new!**
- **Save half of your pocket money for three months and see how much you collect!**

Final Words

Money isn't just about buying stuff—it's about making smart choices. And the coolest part? The better you get at handling money now, the easier it will be when you're older. **You're already leveling up!** 🚀

Jump to chapter 13 If your dad is NOT around

CHAPTER 12
MY DAD'S HERE... BUT EVERY DAD IS DIFFERENT!

So, your dad is in your life—cool! But here's the thing: **Dads come in different "player modes."**

Some dads are like **Co-Op Mode Players** 🎮—they're right there with you, playing alongside you, giving advice, and cracking dad jokes that make you groan but secretly love.

Other dads are more like **Background NPCs (Non-Player Characters)** 🕹—they're around, but they don't say much about *the deep stuff*.

And guess what? **Both are totally okay!**

Dad Mode 1: The Super Engaged Player 🏆

This dad **talks, listens, gives advice**, and might even **try to be "cool"** (...we love the effort, right?) He's the type to ask, *"Hey, how was your day?"* or *"What are you thinking about?"*

- ✔ **Pros:** You get guidance, jokes, and maybe a fun teacher for life skills like fixing a bike or grilling the perfect burger.
- ✘ **Challenges:** He *might* give long speeches when all you wanted was a yes/no answer! 😄

💡 **How to Level Up With This Dad:**

- Appreciate the effort—he's trying to help!
- Ask him to teach you cool stuff (he probably loves sharing random knowledge).
- If he gives a long answer, just **nod and absorb the useful parts** (trust me, there's always something helpful in there).

Dad Mode 2: The Silent Guardian 🤐

This dad is **around but doesn't say much about emotions, puberty, or "awkward" stuff.** Maybe he shows love by doing things rather than saying them.

- ✔ **Pros:** He's steady, reliable, and probably **always there when you need him.**
- ✘ **Challenges:** He might not naturally talk about things like **crushes, feelings, or body changes**—not because he doesn't care, but because **he might not know how.**

💡 **How to Level Up With This Dad:**

- **Give him side quests!** 🕹️ Instead of asking, *"Can we talk about feelings?"* (which might make him glitch 😅), try:
    - ◇ *"Hey Dad, did you ever have a weird growth spurt as a kid?"*
    - ◇ *"What's something you wish someone had told you when you were my age?"*
    - ◇ *"Do you think aliens are real?"* (Okay, this isn't puberty-related, but it gets the convo flowing!)
- **Watch for how he shows love.** Maybe he fixes things, makes sure you eat well, or quietly checks in. Actions speak louder than words!

Bonus Cheat Code: Talking to Dad Without Making It Weird

If talking to your dad feels awkward, here are some **tricks to make it easier:**

🎮 **The Side-by-Side Method:** **Dads often talk better while doing something else.** Try chatting while:

- **Driving** (he's trapped—he has to listen! 😅)
- **Playing a game** (co-op mode = chill conversation)
- **Walking the dog or fixing something together**

📝 **The Shortcut Option:** If talking is too much, write him a **note, text, or email** with your question. Dads sometimes process things better that way.

🕹️ **The Save Game Approach:** If the convo feels awkward, **pause and come back later.** You don't have to talk about everything all at once!

Final Thought: No One Dad Is the Same—And That's Okay!

Some dads talk, some dads don't. Some are goofy, some are serious. Some give **long motivational speeches** while others just **pat you on the back and say "You're good, kid."**

The trick is to **meet your dad where he's at** and **appreciate the way he shows up**—even if it's different from what you expected.

And hey, if you ever need a chat and **dad's in Silent Mode**, remember—you've got a whole **team** of trusted adults who can help. **You're never alone in this game!**

CHAPTER 13
GROWING UP WITHOUT A FATHER – FINDING YOUR OWN ROLE MODELS

You're Not Alone

Many boys grow up without a father in their lives. Some dads **choose to leave**, while others **pass away**. No matter the reason, it's okay to have **big feelings** about it—sadness, anger, confusion, or even just feeling *different* from other kids. You might wonder why it happened, or you might not think about it much at all.

Whatever you feel, **it's normal**, and you are **not alone**.

It's NOT Your Fault

One of the biggest things to understand is this **your dad's absence is NOT your fault.**

Boys often ask themselves:

> **?** Did I do something wrong?
>
> **?** If I had been different, would he have stayed?

The answer is **NO**. Grown-ups make their own choices, and those choices are about *them*, not *you*. Whether your father left by choice or passed away, **his absence does not define your worth**.

Your Parents' Relationship Was Successful—Even If It Didn't Last

Maybe you wonder: *Was their relationship a failure?*

NOPE! Here's why:

> ✔ Their relationship gave **YOU** life.
>
> ✔ That makes it **100% a success**.

It doesn't matter if they stayed together or not. What matters is that **you are here**, and that means **they created something amazing—you!**

When Your Dad Has Passed Away (in memory to my friend Aaron Nable)

Losing a father is a different kind of pain. You might feel like there's a **hole in your life** that no one else can fill. You may miss him even if you didn't get the chance to know him well.

- It's okay to **be sad** and **wish he were here**.
- It's okay to **be angry** that life took him too soon.
- It's okay to **feel numb** or not know how to feel at all.

However you feel, **your emotions are valid**. Talking to someone you trust—your mum, a grandparent, or a mentor—can help.

Honouring Your Father's Memory

Even though he's not here, you can still carry him with you.

💭 **Talk about him** – Ask family members to share stories.

📝 **Write him a letter** – Say what's on your mind, even if he can't read it.

🎨 **Create something in his memory** – A drawing, a poem, or even a small tradition in his honour.

Your dad is part of your story, and you can choose **how to keep his memory alive in a way that feels right for you**.

Finding Healthy Male Role Models

Just because your father isn't around doesn't mean you don't have strong, supportive people in your life. Role models can be:

👨‍🏫 A teacher who encourages you

- 🏆 A coach who pushes you to do your best
- 👴 A grandfather who shares his wisdom
- 🦸 A character from a book or movie who inspires you
- 👥 An uncle or family friend who listens and gives advice

The important thing is to **choose people who make you feel safe, respected, and encouraged**.

What Makes a Good Role Model?

A good role model is someone who:

- ✔ Treats others with kindness and fairness
- ✔ Takes responsibility for their actions
- ✔ Stays positive even when life is hard
- ✔ Stands up for what is right

Look for these qualities in the people around you, and remember—you can **become** a great role model for someone else, too.

Your Dad's Legacy Lives in You

Here's something powerful to remember: **You are the greatest legacy your father has left in this world.** Even if he's not around, a part of him is in you.

But here's the best part—you **get to decide** how that part of him grows. His choices are not yours to carry. **You are your own person.**

Letting Go of Resentment

It's easy to feel angry or hurt when your father isn't in your life. Maybe you wish things were different. Maybe you wonder what life would be like if he were still here. These feelings are **completely normal**.

But holding onto resentment is like carrying a heavy backpack everywhere you go—it only weighs **you** down. **Letting go doesn't mean forgetting. It means freeing yourself to move forward.**

A Meditation for Letting Go

Find a quiet place, take a deep breath, and read this slowly.

"Dad, I let go of the expectations I had about you. You don't owe me anything, and I don't owe you anything either. I free myself from all the expectations you had about me, too. Your choices are your responsibility, and my choices are mine. I will grow and succeed with the part of you that lives in me."

Breathe deeply and imagine yourself **standing strong and free**. You are **enough, just as you are**

CHAPTER 14

BUILDING A STRONG RELATIONSHIP WITH MUM & OTHER SUPPORTIVE PEOPLE

Your Mum's Got This – You Don't Have to Be the Grown-Up!

Sometimes, when a dad isn't around, it can feel like you need to **step up** and take care of your mum. Maybe you've heard her say she's tired, or maybe you just **want to protect her** because you love her.

But guess what? **That's NOT your job!**

Your mum is the **big one** here. She's a grown-up, and **she knows how to take care of herself**. It was *grandma and grandpa's* job to look after her when she was a kid, just like it's **her job to take care of you now**.

Your job? **To be a kid.** To laugh, learn, explore, and enjoy life!

💡 **Think of it like a video game**—if you were given a ticket to play the best game ever, would you spend the whole time worrying about the person who gave it to you? Nope! You'd **jump in, play your best, and enjoy the adventure**. Well, life is your game, and your **mum gave you the ticket**. Now it's time to play!

Finding Other Trusted Adults to Support You

Even though your mum is amazing, **she doesn't have to be the only person you turn to**. Life is full of people who care about you and can **help guide you** when you need it.

Here are some awesome people you can trust:

👴 **Grandparents** – They've seen it all!

👨‍🏫 **Teachers** – They love helping kids figure things out.

🏆 **Coaches** – Great for motivation and advice.

👨‍👦 **Uncles or family friends** – Someone to hang out with and talk to.

📖 **Authors, YouTubers, or role models** – People who inspire you, even from a distance.

If you ever feel **lost, sad, or unsure about something**, remember—you don't have to figure it all out alone.

Love and Support Come in Different Forms

Some boys think, *"If I don't have a dad, I'm missing something."*

But here's the truth: **Love isn't just about having a dad.** Love comes from **so many different places**—your mum, your family, your friends, even people you haven't met yet.

- 🫶 **Love is when someone listens to you.**
- 🫶 **Love is when someone shows up for you.**
- 🫶 **Love is when someone believes in you.**

You are **not alone.** You are **wanted.** You **belong.**

Final Thought – Get Your Ticket to Life!

Imagine life is the **coolest amusement park ever** 🎢. Your parents gave you the ticket, but **you get to decide how to enjoy the ride**.

So go out there, **have fun**, be **kind to yourself**, and remember:

- ⭐ **You are amazing.**
- ⭐ **You belong.**
- ⭐ **You are loved.**

🚀 What Kind of Awesome Dude Are You?

💡 Find out what makes you awesome! Answer these questions, and at the end, count your answers to discover your 'Awesome Type'!

8. What's your favourite way to spend free time?

A. Playing sports or running around outside

B. Drawing, writing, or creating cool projects

C. Playing video games or solving puzzles

D. Hanging out with friends and making people laugh

2. If a friend is feeling down, what do you do?

A. Try to cheer them up with something fun

B. Listen carefully and give them advice

C. Help them figure out a solution to their problem

D. Make a joke or do something silly to lighten their mood

3. If you had to choose a superpower, what would it be?

A. Super strength – because action is awesome

B. Mind reading – so I can understand people better

C. Time travel – so I can plan everything perfectly

D. Shapeshifting – because turning into anything would be hilarious

WHAT KIND OF AWESOME DUDE ARE YOU?

4. What's your dream job?

A. A pro athlete, firefighter, or astronaut

B. An artist, musician, or writer

C. A scientist, engineer, or inventor

D. A comedian, YouTuber, or talk show host

6. What's your biggest strength?

A. I'm brave and always up for a challenge

B. I'm thoughtful and creative

C. I'm smart and good at figuring things out

D. I'm funny and make people happy

Results:

⭐ **Mostly A's - The Action Hero:** You love adventure, excitement, and being active! You're a natural leader and always up for a challenge.

🎨 **Mostly B's - The Creative Genius:** Your imagination is amazing! You see the world in unique ways and bring cool ideas to life.

🤔 **Mostly C's - The Problem Solver:** You love figuring things out and making plans. You think before acting and always look for the best solutions.

😄 **Mostly D's - The Fun Master:** You're the life of the party! You make people laugh and know how to bring positive vibes wherever you go.

🦉 How Well Do You Know Yourself?

💡 Answer "Yes" or "No" to these questions. The more "Yes" answers you have, the better you understand yourself!

1. Do you know what makes you happy and what makes you upset?
2. Can you tell when you're getting stressed or overwhelmed?
3. Do you have a way to calm yourself down when you're feeling upset?
4. Do you know what your biggest strengths are?
5. Do you know what your biggest challenges are and how to work on them?
6. Do you get how your actions can make someone feel awesome... or not so great?
7. Can you recognize when you need help and ask for it?
8. Do you have hobbies or things that you love doing?
9. Can you name at least three people you trust and can talk to?
10. Do you feel good about yourself most of the time?

📝 Score Yourself:

- 8-10 Yes answers – You know yourself really well! That's a superpower!
- 5-7 Yes answers – You're on the right path, but there's still room to explore.
- 0-4 Yes answers – Time to level up your self-knowledge! Pay more attention to your feelings and thoughts.

Here's how to start leveling up:

- Pick one trusted adult or friend and have a chat about how you're feeling this week.
- Keep a "Mood Journal" for a week—write down one thing that made you happy and one thing that upset you every day. You'll start noticing patterns and understanding yourself better!

🎮 Level Up Your Life Game

💡 **Complete these challenges and tick them off as you go. Each one gets you closer to the next "level" in life!**

🎯 LEVEL 1: Daily Wins

- [ ] I said "thank you" today
- [ ] I helped someone without being asked
- [ ] I tried something new
- [ ] I drank water instead of soda/juice
- [ ] I ate fruits/veggies instead of chocolates/chips
- [ ] I did something kind for myself

🎯 LEVEL 2: Growing Strong

- [ ] I made my bed or cleaned up my space
- [ ] took a deep breath instead of getting mad right away
- [ ] I finished a task even when it was hard
- [ ] I did something active (like a sport, bike ride, or a walk)
- [ ] I said something nice to someone

🎯 LEVEL 3: Super Star Skills

- [ ] I apologised when I made a mistake
- [ ] I asked for help when I needed it
- [ ] I told someone how I felt instead of keeping it inside
- [ ] I tried to see things from someone else's point of view
- [ ] I persisted, even when it was tough

🏆 Final Level: Boss Mode!

- ☐ I stood up for myself or for someone else in a kind way
- ☐ I helped a friend or family member with something important
- ☐ I talked to an adult when something didn't feel right
- ☐ I learned from a mistake instead of feeling bad about it
- ☐ I felt proud of myself for something I did today!

🎉 **Once you've completed all the levels, you're officially in BOSS MODE!**

😄 Crush-O-Meter: How Big Is Your Crush?

💡 **Answer the questions and see where you land on the Crush-O-Meter!**

1. You see your crush at school. What do you do?

A. Say "Hey" like a normal person. No big deal.

B. Try to act cool but somehow trip over nothing.

C. Forget how to use words and just nod weirdly.

2. Your friends mention your crush's name. What happens?

A. Nothing, why? I'm totally chill.

B. I feel my face heat up, and I quickly check my phone to pretend I don't care.

C. I panic and accidentally spill my drink all over myself.

3. Your crush sends you a text. How do you respond?

A. Quickly and casually. No stress.

B. Take 30 minutes to draft the perfect response.

C. Throw my phone across the room and happy-scream into a pillow.

4. Your crush laughs at your joke. What's your reaction?

A. Smile. Cool, they have good taste.

B. Overanalyse if they were laughing with me or at me.

C. Immediately plan our future wedding in my head.

Results:

★ **Mostly A's – The Chill Dude**: You've got a crush, but you're keeping it cool. Respect.

😄 **Mostly B's – The Slightly Awkward Admirer**: You're feeling the butterflies, but don't worry—it's totally normal!

🌪 **Mostly C's – The Walking Disaster**: We see you. We feel you. Deep breaths. You got this.

🏆 Friendship Decoder: Who's Really Got Your Back?

Not all friends are the same! Some are the best kind of people, while others... well, let's just say they might not be on your *dream team*. Use this Friendship Decoder to figure out who's really got your back and how to be a great friend yourself!

🦉 Step 1: Spot the Friend Types

💡 Which of these sounds like someone you know?

- **The Loyal Legend** – Always has your back, cheers you on, and keeps your secrets safe. 💯
- *The Fun One* – Makes you laugh until your stomach hurts. Never a boring moment. 😂
- **The Wise One** – Gives solid advice and helps you think before you act. 💭
- **The Fair-Weather Friend** – Nice when things are fun, but disappears when you need support. 🏃
- **The Tease** – Jokes at you instead of with you. Sometimes, it doesn't feel funny. 😐
- **The Drama King/Queen** – Loves gossip and making small things a big deal. 🎭
- **The Secret Betrayer** – Pretends to be your friend but talks behind your back. 🚩

☞ **Good friends make you feel happy, supported, and like you can be yourself.**

☞ **Not-so-great friends make you feel stressed, left out, or like you have to change who you are.**

🏆 Step 2: The Friendship Test

💡 Answer YES or NO to these questions:

1. Do I feel good about myself when I'm with this friend?
2. Can I trust them to keep my secrets and stand up for me?
3. Do they listen when I talk, not just wait for their turn?
4. If I make a mistake, do they help me fix it instead of making fun of me?
5. Are they happy for me when something good happens, or do they get jealous?
6. 6-Do they encourage me to make good choices, or do they pressure me to do things I don't want to?
7. If I had a problem, would I feel comfortable asking them for help?

🔴 **If you answered YES to most of these, congrats! You've got a solid friend.**

🚨 **If you answered NO to a lot of them, you might need to rethink if this person is really a good friend.**

🤝 Step 3: Leveling Up Your Friendship Game

Want to be a great friend? Here's how to Level Up:

- ✔ **Be Reliable** – Show up when you say you will. Keep promises.
- ✔ **Respect Boundaries** – Friends need space too!
- ✔ **Support, Don't Compete** – Cheer them on instead of trying to outdo them.
- ✔ **Apologise When Needed** – If you mess up, own it, and fix it.
- ✔ **Be a Friend, Not a Judge** – No one's perfect. Accept your friends for who they are.

⚡ Final Boss Battle: The Fake Friend Dilemma

💡 **What do you do if someone isn't a great friend?**

📱 **Option 1: Walk Away** – If they're treating you badly, you don't have to stay friends. Find your *real* people.

🗣 **Option 2: Speak Up** – If they're a decent person but making mistakes, talk to them. "Hey, I didn't like when you [did that thing]. Can we be better friends to each other?"

💡 **Option 3: Know Your Worth** – You deserve friends who respect you. If someone isn't treating you right, don't waste your time trying to change them. Find your *real* team.

😎 **Remember: A good friend makes life better. A bad friend makes life harder. Choose wisely!**

🎒 Friendship Emergency Kit: What to Do When Things Get Messy

Friendships are awesome... until they're not. Arguments, misunderstandings, and awkward moments happen to everyone. But don't panic! Here's your **Friendship Emergency Kit** to help you handle tricky situations like a pro.

🚨 Problem #1: My Friend and I Had a Big Fight

What's Happening?

Maybe they said something hurtful, or maybe you got mad and yelled at them. Now, things are weird.

How to Fix It:

- ✔ **Cool Off First** – Take a deep breath before reacting.
- ✔ **Think About What Happened** – Was it a misunderstanding? Was anyone wrong?
- ✔ **Talk It Out** – Say, "Hey, I don't want us to stay mad. Can we talk?"
- ✔ **Apologize If Needed** – If you messed up, own it. "I'm sorry for what I said."
- ✔ **Forgive & Move On** – If they're sorry too, don't hold a grudge.

😯 Problem #2: I Feel Left Out

What's Happening?

Your friends are hanging out without you, and you're not sure why.

How to Handle It:

💡 **Step 1: Check the Facts** – Maybe it wasn't personal. Did they plan it without thinking?

💡 **Step 2: Speak Up** – If it keeps happening, ask, "Hey, I noticed I haven't been invited much. Is everything okay?"

💡 **Step 3: Make New Connections** – Don't wait around. Find other people to hang with.

🚨 **Warning Sign:** If they *always* leave you out on purpose, they might not be real friends. Find your tribe!

🗣 **Problem #3: My Friend Keeps Teasing Me**

What's Happening?

It started as a joke, but now it feels mean.

What to Do:

- **Be Direct** – "Hey, that's not funny to me."
- **Set a Boundary** – If they don't stop, say, "I'm not okay with that. Cut it out."
- **Walk Away** – If they don't respect you, they're not a real friend.

😎 **Power Move:** Real friends make you laugh, not feel bad. Know the difference!

👀 Problem #4: My Friend Is Acting Different

What's Happening?

They used to be fun, but now they seem angry, distant, or not themselves.

What You Can Do:

- **Check In** – "Hey, you seem different lately. Is everything okay?"
- **Listen** – Sometimes, people just need to talk.
- **Support Them** – If they're struggling, remind them they're not alone.

🚨 **If they're really upset, you can talk to a trusted adult about your worries.**

⏳ Bonus Level: Making New Friends

Feeling like you need a new squad? Try this:

- **Start a Conversation** – "Hey, I like your shirt. Where'd you get it?"
- **Join a Club or Sport** – Instant way to meet new people.
- **Find Your Kind of Funny** – People who laugh at the same stuff usually click.
- **Be Open** – The best friends might not be the ones you expect!
- **Final Rule:** A good friend makes life better, not worse. Surround yourself with people who bring out the best in you!

🏆 What Kind of Friend Are You?

Ever wonder what type of friend you are? Take this fun quiz to find out!

1. **Your friend is upset because they lost a big game. What do you do?**
   A. Give them a pep talk and remind them they'll crush it next time.
   B. Listen and let them vent—sometimes, they just need to talk.
   C. Make a joke to brighten up their mood.
   D. Challenge them to a rematch and help them improve.

2. **Your friend forgets your birthday. How do you react?**
   A. No big deal—I know they care about me.
   B. I feel a little hurt but talk to them about it in a respectful way.
   C. Joke that they owe me double the gifts next year.
   D. Plan something fun anyway—birthdays are about celebrating, not gifts.

3. **Someone is being mean to your friend. What's your move?**
   A. Stand up for them and tell the person to back off.
   B. Check in with my friend later and see if they're okay.
   C. Come up with a clever comeback to shut the bully down.
   D. Remind my friend that one mean person doesn't define them.

4. **Your friend is struggling with a tough decision. How do you help?**

A. Give them solid advice based on what I'd do.

B. Ask them questions to help them figure it out.

C. Help them see the funny side to take off the pressure.

D. Remind them they can handle anything and support their choice.

5. **How do you usually make new friends?**

A. I start talking to people and see who clicks.

B. I look for people who share my interests.

C. I make them laugh—humour is my superpower.

D. I don't force it—good friendships happen naturally.

✷ Results: What Kind of Friend Are You?

Mostly A's: The Leader 🏆

You're the one who always has a plan and looks out for your friends. People trust you to take charge and help them out.

Mostly B's: The Listener 👂

You're the friend everyone turns to when they need advice or just someone to hear them out. Your kindness makes people feel safe.

Mostly C's: The Jokester 😄

You keep things fun and know how to make people laugh, even when things get tough. Just make sure your jokes don't cross the line.

Mostly D's: The Motivator 🚀

You inspire your friends to be the best version of themselves. You always have their backs and remind them they can do anything.

No matter what type of friend you are, the best friendships are built on kindness, honesty, and fun! 😎

Here's a fun and engaging development of your **Cool Printable Activities** section!

📃 Cool Printable Activities

- **Design Your Own Superhero**
- **What's your superhero name?**
- **What's your special power?** (Helping others? Standing up for friends? Telling the best jokes?)
- **What's your superhero costume like?** (Cape? Cool sneakers? A mask?)
- **What's your hero's motto?** ("I always try my best!" "Kindness is my superpower!")
- **Who is your hero's biggest challenge or enemy?** (Self-doubt? The 'mean thoughts monster'?)

💡 **Bonus Challenge:** Draw a picture of your superhero self and write a mini comic strip about your adventures!

🎟️ My Life Ticket

Your **Life Ticket** is your **reminder that you belong, matter, and can create an awesome future!**

🎟️ **Name:** _____

🎟️ **Age:** _____

🎟️ **Special Abilities:** _____

🎟️ **I Belong Because…** _____

🎟️ **One Thing I'm Proud Of:** _____

🎟️ **One Big Dream I Have:** _____

💡 **Bonus Challenge:** Decorate your ticket with stickers, drawings, or fun colours and put it somewhere you'll see it every day!

💌 The Future Me Letter

Write a letter to your future self—one you can open in **one year, three years, or even when you're a teenager!**

Dear Future Me,

Right now, I am ___ years old.

Some things I love are _____.

Something I'm really good at is _____.

One thing I want to get better at is _____.

When I grow up, I hope I _____.

I want to remind myself that _____.

No matter what happens, I hope I always _____.

From,

(Your name)

💡 **Bonus Challenge:** Seal this letter in an envelope and write on the front: **"Do not open until [pick a future date]!"** Hide it in a safe place or give it to a trusted adult to keep for you.

🎲 Family System Domino Effect Game

This fun and meaningful activity helps boys **visualize their family system** and **understand the flow of life** from their ancestors to them. It's a simple but powerful way to explore where they come from and how they belong.

🎯 How to Play:

1. **Print or Draw** the Family System Domino Cards. Each domino has two spaces—one for a name and one for a connection.

2. **Fill in the blanks** with the names of family members, starting from the **great-grandparents** down to **yourself**. If you don't know some names, leave them blank or write something like "A kind man/woman who helped create my family."

3. **Line up the dominoes** in order, showing how life passed through generations to **YOU!**

4. **Decorate & Customize** – Add drawings, stickers, or fun facts about each family member.

🎏 Family System Domino Cards

[1] **Great-Grandparents** → Passed on life to → **Grandparents**

🖊 **Names:** _____ & _____

[2] **Grandparents** → Passed on life to → **Parents**

🖊 **Names:** _____ & _____

[3] **Parents** → Passed on life to → **Me!**

🖊 **Names:** _____ & _____

[4] **Me!** → I am part of my family tree, and I belong!

💡 Bonus Activity:

🌳 **Create Your Family Tree:** Draw a big tree and write each family member's name on a branch. Add yourself at the bottom to show that **you are the newest, strongest branch!**

⌛ **Superpower Reflection:** Write down **one strength** you think was passed down to you from each generation. Example:

- **Great-grandparents**: Hardworking spirit
- **Grandparents**: Love for music
- **Parents**: Good at solving problems
- **Me**: A mix of all their strengths!

www.ingramcontent.com/pod-product-compliance
Lightning Source LLC
Chambersburg PA
CBHW071903070526
44583CB00016B/1827